3.13

	DATE DUE		
APR 13 2019			

BL: 5.6   AR: 0.5 Pt   123710

TRAP AND SKEET SHOOTING

FOR FUN!

by Shane Frederick

Content Adviser: Jim Shulind, Certified Hunter Education/Firearms Safety Instructor,
State of North Dakota, Grand Forks, North Dakota
Reading Adviser: Susan Kesselring, M.A., Literacy Educator, Rosemount-Apple Valley-Eagan (Minnesota) School District

Compass Point Books ✦ Minneapolis, Minnesota

Compass Point Books
151 Good Counsel Drive
P.O. Box 669
Mankato, MN 56002-0669

This book was manufactured with paper containing at least 10 percent post-consumer waste.

Photographs ©: SawayaPhoto/iStockphoto, front cover (left); Bobby Deal/RealDealPhoto/Shutterstock, front cover (right), back cover, 8-9, 15 (bottom), 42 (left); AP Images, 4-5, 31; Jack Scrivener/Shutterstock, 5 (right); Private Collection/Photo ©Bonhams, London, U.K./The Bridgeman Art Library, 6 (bottom); Joe Fox/Alamy, 6-7 (top); John E. Fletcher/National Geographic/Getty Images, 7 (right); AP Images/*Alamogordo Daily News*/Ellis Neel, 9 (right); Jason Lugo/iStockphoto, 10 (left); Konjushenko Vladimir Iljich/Shutterstock, 10-11; Tim Wright/Corbis, 12-13 (bottom); Wallenrock/Shutterstock, 12-13 (top), 47; Jackson Gee/Shutterstock, 14; Clark Brennan/Alamy, 15 (top); Howard Sears/Shutterstock, 16; David Kennedy/Art Life Images, 17; Milos Bicanski/Getty Images, 18-19; Stacey Lynn Brown/Shutterstock, 19 (right); Jana Thompson/Alamy, 20; casper/iStockphoto, 21; William Leaman/Alamy, 22, 27 (right); LeCajun/Shutterstock, 23; Chandler Hall/Shutterstock, 24-25 (front); Gary Detonnancourt/Shutterstock, 24-25 (back); Paul Brennan/Shutterstock, 26-27; Robert Laberge/Getty Images, 28, 33; Popperfoto/Getty Images, 29; Alex Mita/AFP/Getty Images, 30-31; China Photos/Getty Images, 32; Bettmann/Corbis, 34-35; Dwight D. Eisenhower Library, 35; AP Images/Al Behrman, 36; AP Images/*News-Democrat*/Derik Holtmann, 37; Keystone/Getty Images, 38; James L. Amos/Corbis, 39; David Umberger/Purdue University, 40; Lindenwood University, 41; 2008 Jupiterimages Corporation, 42 (right); Paul Brennan/Dreamstime.com, 43 (left); BigStockPhoto.com, 43 (right); R. Gates/Hulton Archive/Getty Images, 44; Hugo de Wolf/Shutterstock, 45.

Editor: Brenda Haugen
Page Production: The Design Lab
Photo Researcher: Robert McConnell
Art Director: LuAnn Ascheman-Adams
Creative Director: Keith Griffin
Editorial Director: Nick Healy
Managing Editor: Catherine Neitge

Library of Congress Cataloging-in-Publication Data
Frederick, Shane.
  Trap and skeet shooting for fun! / by Shane Frederick.
     p. cm. — (For fun!)
  Includes index.
  ISBN 978-0-7565-3865-1 (library binding)
1. Trapshooting—Juvenile literature.
2. Skeet shooting—Juvenile literature. I. Title. II. Series.
  GV1181.F74 2009
  799.3'132—dc22   2008009865

Ingram 3/13   26.65

Visit Compass Point Books on the Internet at *www.compasspointbooks.com*
or e-mail your request to *custserv@compasspointbooks.com*

Table of Contents

Note: In this book, there are two kinds of vocabulary words. Shooting Words to Know are words specific to trap and skeet shooting. They are defined on page 46. Other Words to Know are helpful words that are not related only to trap and skeet shooting. They are defined on page 47.

On Target

When you see a target, do you get the urge to hit it? Whether you're shooting a basketball at a hoop or throwing a ball at a glove, it's fun to test your aim.

People have been shooting guns at targets for hundreds of years. At first, the targets were animals being hunted. Then people began aiming at other objects made of wood, glass, or paper. Some shot at these targets as practice for hunting. Others did it just for fun.

4

One great challenge was trying to hit moving targets, such as birds. That's how the sports of trap shooting and skeet shooting were born.

Today millions of people shoot at moving targets called clay pigeons. Some people shoot in competitions and dream of going to the Olympics. Others shoot as a hobby and do it with family, friends, and classmates.

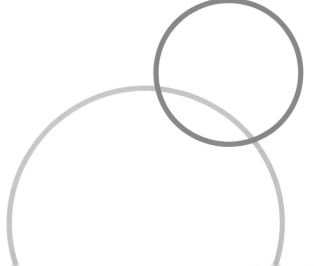

An Old Sport

The sport of trap shooting started in England more than 200 years ago. Live birds were shot as they were released from hats or boxes called traps. The sport spread around the world.

In time, people who played the sport decided to shoot at flying targets rather than killing real birds. They tried shooting glass balls, tin birds, and clay disks. All these objects were launched out of traps. Shooters liked the clay disks

6

Stacks of clay pigeons

best. These disks moved through the air more like birds, unlike the other objects. They called these targets clay pigeons. Some people still call them that today. Others just call them clays. Despite their name, these targets are usually made out of pitch and limestone dust.

Hunted to Extinction

The passenger pigeon was a wild bird that was used for trap shooting in North America during the 1700s and 1800s. The bird became extinct because of so much hunting.

A stuffed passenger pigeon is on display at a museum.

One Trap or Two?

Trap shooting and skeet shooting are similar, but they're not the same sport. Both sports use shotguns and clay pigeons. But each sport is played differently and has its own rules.

A clay pigeon is ready for launch.

Clay pigeons are released for a shooter in La Luz, New Mexico.

In trap shooting, the clay pigeons fly out of one trap and away from the shooters. In skeet shooting, the targets are launched from two separate trap houses and fly across the field in front of the shooters. Skeet was invented in the 1920s as a game that was more like wild bird hunting than trap shooting was.

Funny Name

Skeet is an old Scandinavian word that means "shoot."

Practice Makes Perfect

Some people shoot trap and skeet to sharpen their bird-hunting skills. People like to hunt many game birds, such as pheasants, grouse, quail, ducks, and geese.

A hunter aimed at a pheasant.

A grouse hunter named Charles E. Davies of Andover, Massachusetts, invented the sport of skeet in the 1920s. This new sport offered a fun way to get ready for the hunting season. Now at any time of the year, skeet shooters could practice shooting their guns at many different angles to improve their aims.

Get Ready to Hunt

Since most hunting seasons begin in the fall, summer is a popular time of year to shoot trap and skeet.

Choose Your Weapon

There are many different kinds of guns. There are rifles, pistols, and shotguns. Shotguns are often used to hunt game birds and other small animals. Shotguns also are used in trap and skeet shooting.

Instead of bullets, shotguns shoot shells, cartridges filled with pellets called shot. After the shotgun is fired, the pellets spread out to cover a wide area. This makes it easier to hit small targets.

A 12-gauge shotgun, shotgun shells, and clay pigeons

Shotgun shells are filled with little round pellets.

There are different sizes of shot. The smallest is birdshot. The biggest is buckshot. Although almost any style and gauge of shotgun can be used in trap and skeet, some people have guns that are only used for shooting sports.

Differences in Guns

Rifles and pistols are not used to hunt game birds or to shoot at flying targets. Rifles and pistols shoot single bullets at very high speeds. If shot up into the air, bullets from rifles and pistols can travel up to 3 miles (4.8 kilometers). Shotgun pellets travel about 100 yards (91 meters). Rifles and pistols should never be shot up into the air because you don't know where the bullet will land.

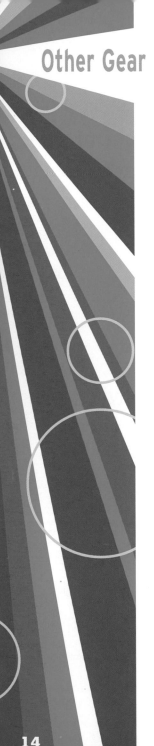

More Items You Will Need

Trap and skeet shooters can wear almost any kind of comfortable clothes. It's good to have warm, waterproof jackets handy in case of bad weather. Sturdy shoes or boots also are good to have.

Other gear that shooters need includes:

Eye protection: Glasses, sunglasses, or safety glasses with side guards can save your eyes from falling shots, broken target chips, or a gun that doesn't function correctly.

Ear protection: Earplugs or earmuffs protect your ears from a gun's blast. Loud noises can cause hearing loss, so hearing protection is important. Most shooting clubs and ranges require shooters to wear ear and eye protection.

Vest: A vest with big pockets is useful. Shooters often have one pocket for unused shotgun shells and another for used ones.

Pull!

When live birds used for trap shooting flew out of their boxes, shooters didn't know where the birds were going to fly. In American trap, shooters still don't know where the targets are going to go. The clay pigeons are released from a machine that moves back and forth so the targets fly out at different angles. It also releases the clay pigeons 10 feet (3 m) off the ground.

In singles trap, each person shoots from five different stations located 16 yards (14.6 m) from the trap. He or she takes five shots at each station before moving on to the next one. A shooter gets a perfect score if all 25 targets in the round are broken.

In handicap trap shooting, a person shoots from greater distances, depending on how good he or she is. The best shooters may shoot from as far as 27 yards (24.7 m) behind the trap.

Another version of trap is doubles. In that game, two targets are thrown at the same time. Shooters fire once at each target from the five different stations. The trap does not rotate back and forth. A perfect score is 50.

Ready to Launch
Shooters call for the targets to be launched. The most common call is "Pull!" because the targets were launched by pulling a lever. Now many clubs use voice-activated launchers.

A Different Challenge

In skeet shooting, targets are launched out of two "houses." One is a high house that fires the clay pigeons from 10 feet (3 m) off the ground. The other is a low house that launches the birds from 3 feet (91 centimeters) off the ground.

People take shots from eight different stations. The first seven stations are set in a half circle between the two houses. The eighth station is halfway between the houses. The houses launch

a total of 25 targets in a round. At each station, each house launches one target at a time, with the high house shooting first. At stations 1, 2, 6, and 7, however, two more clays are launched at the same time.

Game Change
Originally skeet was played on a full circle instead of a semicircle. The shooters fired from 12 different spots around the circle, so it was called "around the clock."

Golf With a Shotgun

Sporting clays is a shooting game that is even more like being out on a hunt.

Sporting clays is sometimes called "golf with a shotgun," because people who play it walk a course just like golfers do. In sporting clays, people take shots at many different stations. No two courses are alike.

The targets come in several sizes and are launched at different speeds and angles. Some targets are thrown high in the air like flying ducks or geese. Some roll or bounce on the ground like rabbits.

Sporting clays is more challenging than trap or skeet. However, beginners like it as much as the more experienced players do.

Games Galore!

There are other clay-target games, too. "Down the line" is a version of trap played in England and Australia. Wobble traps fire clay targets at different heights as well as in different directions. "Five stand" is a game similar to sporting clays, but it is not spread out on a course.

Follow the Rules

Shooting trap and skeet can be lots of fun. But guns are very dangerous and must be handled with care.

You must learn how to use shotguns safely before you try clay-target sports.

Parents and other family members who shoot often teach their children how to use firearms. State and local conservation departments often offer classes on safety and gun use.

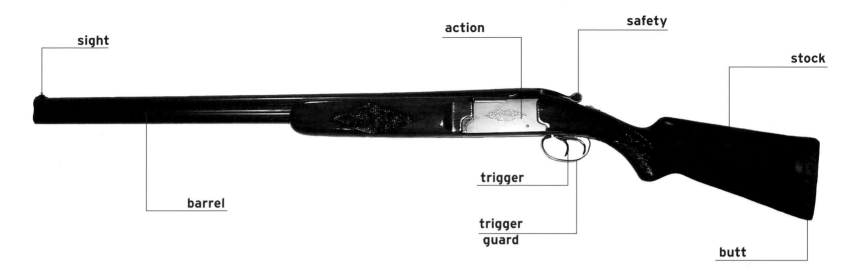

sight

action

safety

stock

barrel

trigger

trigger guard

butt

Some rules you should know:

- An adult should be with you at all times whenever you handle a firearm.

- When you're at the shooting range, always keep the action of your gun open and your gun unloaded until you reach the station and it is your turn to shoot.

- Always know what's behind or around your target before you shoot.

- Keep the barrel of your gun pointed in a safe direction at all times, even if you think it's not loaded.

- Keep your finger outside the trigger guard until you are ready to shoot.

Handle With Care

The most important rule in handling firearms is to treat every gun as if it is loaded.

Taking Your Shot

You may have heard the expression, "Ready, aim, fire!" Shotgun shooters usually don't have time to raise their guns and aim at the fast-moving clay pigeons.

A shooter sets up in the proper stance, puts the gun in the shooting position, and calls for the target. When the clay is launched, a shooter swings his or her gun and points it toward the front of the moving target.

A clay pigeon that has been hit

It's important to keep your eyes on the target. You also must lead—shoot just ahead of your target to allow for the target's movement. After pulling the trigger, swing the gun smoothly all the way through your shot. This is called the follow through.

The first time you see the target break will be a great feeling. Clay-target shooting doesn't take long to learn, but the only way to get better is to practice, practice, practice.

Join the Fun!

To get started shooting trap, skeet, or other clay-pigeon sports, you need to find a shooting club or range near you. Chances are, there will be one. There are more than 2,000 shooting clubs in the United States, and clubs are located in all 50 states. Some states that have more than 100 clubs include Pennsylvania, New York, Michigan, and Minnesota.

Shooting clubs often offer matches and leagues for shooters of all ages and abilities. These clubs sometimes host state and national competitions that are fun to watch. Some clubs also have open times for beginners to try shooting. Some even have coaches and instructors who can teach people how to shoot and play the games.

Going for the Gold

The Olympics aren't just for runners, swimmers, or gymnasts. Trap and skeet shooters can win gold, silver, and bronze medals, too.

E Gao of China competed in women's double trap at the 2004 Olympics.

Shooting has been in the Olympics for more than 100 years. Trap was added as an Olympic sport in 1900 in Paris, France. Skeet was added in 1968 when the Summer Olympics were in Mexico City, Mexico.

Like American trap, the Olympics have an event called double trap. In that game, two clay pigeons are released at the same time, and shooters must try to hit each target with their two shots.

An Old Sport

The modern Olympics began in 1896 in Athens, Greece. Shooting was an event that year, but trap wasn't added until four years later.

Roger de Barbarin of France won the gold medal in men's trap shooting at the 1900 Olympics in Paris, France.

Young Gun

It doesn't matter if you're a girl or a boy, young or old. Clay shooting is for everyone—even at the highest levels.

Vincent Hancock (right) became the best skeet shooter in the world when he was just 16 years old. Hancock competed against adults twice his age, but he won the 2005 International Skeet World Championship in Korea and set three world records.

Hancock began shooting clay pigeons when he was 5 years old. He started shooting in competitions when he was 11. By the time he was in high school, he was practicing shooting every day after school in a field in his back yard. He practiced until it was too dark to shoot. He also exercised to keep his body and mind in shape. Hancock's goal is to win a gold medal in the Olympics.

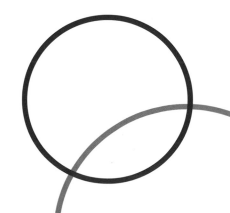

Another Young Champ

In 1936, Dick Shaughnessy, a 14-year-old from Boston, won the National Skeet Championship.

Dick Shaughnessy in 1940

Playing With the Boys

For many years, men and women competed against one another in Olympic and international shooting events. During the 1992 Olympics in Barcelona, Spain, a Chinese woman named Zhang Shan (right) became the first woman to win the gold medal in mixed skeet competition. She set an Olympic record with her performance.

American Kimberley Rhode lined up a shot during the 2004 Olympics.

After Zhang Shan's win, the International Shooting Union barred women from competing against men. Zhang Shan didn't get to defend her gold medal during the 1996 Olympics because there was no event for women. She finally got a chance to shoot in the 2000 Olympics in Sydney, Australia, when a women's skeet event was added. She earned eighth place.

Chance at Olympic Gold

Women have shot trap and skeet for many years, but their first chance to shoot in the Olympics was in 1968.

The President's Private Range

Camp David is a weekend retreat for the president of the United States. The retreat is located in Catoctin Mountain Park in Maryland, just 70 miles (113 km) from the White House in Washington, D.C. Camp David has a swimming pool, tennis courts, horseback riding trails, and a skeet shooting range.

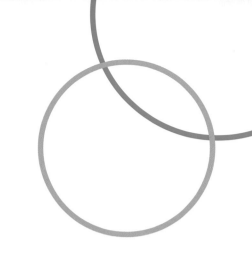

Camp David

President Dwight Eisenhower
skeet shooting at Camp David

Many presidents, including George W. Bush, have shot skeet at Camp David. President Dwight D. Eisenhower enjoyed skeet shooting at Camp David. He named the presidential retreat after his grandson Dwight David Eisenhower. President Eisenhower always tried to improve his shooting skills. He even wrote letters to people asking for advice on how to become a better skeet shooter. In one letter Eisenhower wrote that his best score was 20 of 25 targets.

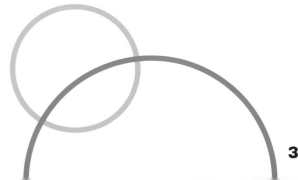

Grand Old Time

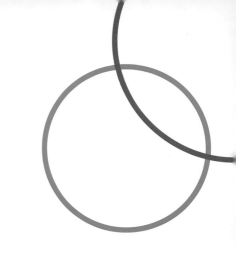

Each August, thousands of trap shooters get together for the Grand American World Trapshooting Championships. It's the largest shooting event in the world and lasts 13 days.

A shooter practiced at the complex in Sparta, Illinois.

The event started in Dexter Park in Long Island, New York, in 1893. It's also been held in Chicago, Illinois, and St. Louis, Missouri. For more than 80 years, it was held in Ohio. Now it takes place at the World Shooting and Recreational Complex in Sparta, Illinois. The complex is the largest of its kind. It has 120 trap fields spread out over 3.5 miles (5.6 km).

The first time the Grand American was held, only 74 people participated. Now almost 6,000 people from all over the country join the shoot. Many people drive recreational vehicles to the complex and camp right at the site.

Annie Got Her Gun

Annie Oakley (right) was a sharpshooter in the late 1800s and early 1900s. She showed off her talents with guns during shows all around the world.

Oakley became one of the most famous women in the United States because of her skills. She shot all kinds of guns and was considered one of the greatest trap shooters of the 1800s.

A Wild Time

Annie Oakley was part of Buffalo Bill's Wild West show, which toured the world.

She once shot 4,722 of 5,000 glass balls released from a trap. She hit 97 of 100 targets at the Grand American in 1925 when she was 65 years old. She died one year later.

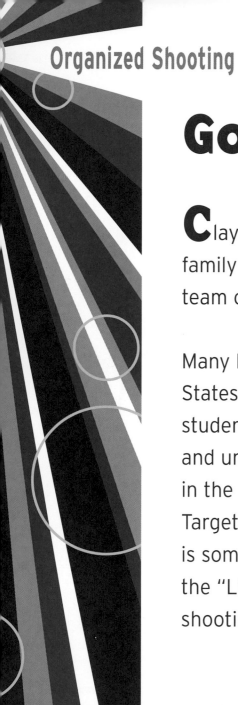

Go, Team, Go!

Clay-target shooting can be a fun activity to do with family members, friends, or by yourself. Being part of a team can be fun, too.

Many high schools and colleges around the United States have shotgun-shooting teams. More than 10,000 students in grades 12 and under compete in the Scholastic Clay Target Program, which is sometimes called the "Little League of shooting sports."

A student practiced as his coach watched.

The 2007 Lindenwood University shooting team

Some colleges offer scholarships for good shooters who agree to compete on their teams. Texas A&M, Purdue, and Yale are among the colleges that have shooting teams. But one little school—Lindenwood University in St. Charles, Missouri—boasts a team that has become a dominant force in recent years. The Lindenwood Lions have won four national championships in a row between 2004 and 2007.

What Happened When?

| 1500 | 1830 | 1880 | 1890 | 1900 | 1910 |

1549 The first mention of hunting small game with a shotgun is put in English law.

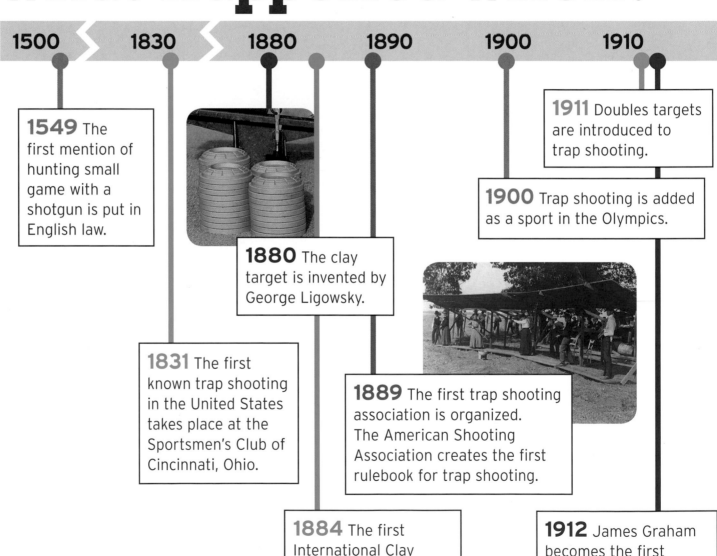

1880 The clay target is invented by George Ligowsky.

1911 Doubles targets are introduced to trap shooting.

1900 Trap shooting is added as a sport in the Olympics.

1831 The first known trap shooting in the United States takes place at the Sportsmen's Club of Cincinnati, Ohio.

1889 The first trap shooting association is organized. The American Shooting Association creates the first rulebook for trap shooting.

1884 The first International Clay Pigeon Tournament is held in Chicago, Illinois.

1912 James Graham becomes the first American to win a gold medal in Olympic trap.

1920 | **1930** | **1940** | **1950** | **1960** | **1980** | **1990** | **2000** | **2010**

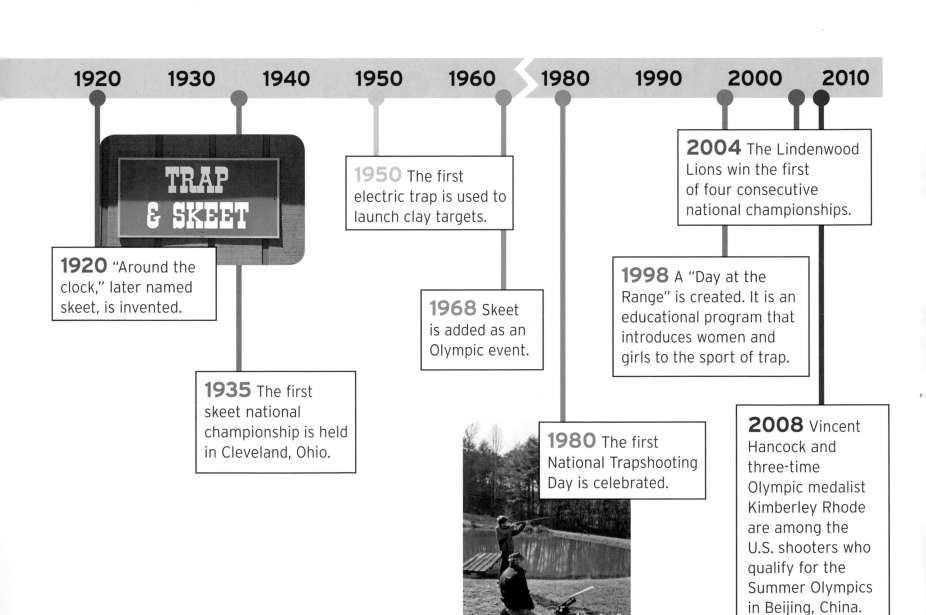

TRAP & SKEET

1950 The first electric trap is used to launch clay targets.

2004 The Lindenwood Lions win the first of four consecutive national championships.

1920 "Around the clock," later named skeet, is invented.

1968 Skeet is added as an Olympic event.

1998 A "Day at the Range" is created. It is an educational program that introduces women and girls to the sport of trap.

1935 The first skeet national championship is held in Cleveland, Ohio.

1980 The first National Trapshooting Day is celebrated.

2008 Vincent Hancock and three-time Olympic medalist Kimberley Rhode are among the U.S. shooters who qualify for the Summer Olympics in Beijing, China.

Fun Trap and Skeet Shooting Facts

Clay targets are about 4 $\frac{3}{10}$ inches (11 cm) in diameter. They're about 1 inch (2.5 cm) thick and weigh less than 4 ounces (113 grams).

In 1926, Gertrude Hurlbutt of Dayton, Montana, won $100 for her suggestion of "skeet" as the name of a new shooting sport.

John Phillip Sousa was the first president of the American Trapshooting Association. Sousa is most famous for writing marching music. One of his most famous songs is "Stars and Stripes Forever."

In 2005, Mike Blaisdell defeated Brian Whalen 575 to 574 in the longest match in trap shooting history. The match in Elysburg, Pennsylvania, had to be stopped at night and resumed the next day. Neither shooter missed a target until Whalen missed his 568th shot. That was in the 23rd round of shooting!

In Olympic trap shooting, clay pigeons fly faster than 70 miles per hour (112.7 kilometers per hour). In U.S. trap and skeet, the targets fly only about 45 mph (72.4 kph).

Trap and skeet rounds have 25 shots because that's how many shells are in a box.

Shooting Words to Know

action: part of a firearm that loads, fires, and removes the empty shotgun shell

gauge: unit of measure for the size of a shotgun barrel

firearm: any kind of gun

follow through: completion of a motion; in shooting it means swinging the gun even after pulling the trigger

houses: places from which clay pigeons are launched during trap and skeet competitions

lead: firing a gun just ahead of the moving target to allow for the movement of the target

mixed: event that has both men and women competing against one another

sharpshooter: person who is highly skilled at shooting guns

shells: cartridges designed for shotguns and filled with shot

shot: small pellets inside a shell

stations: spots where people shoot from in trap and skeet competitions

Other Words to Know

extinct: no longer existing or living

hobby: activity or interest that people do for fun

pitch: dark, sticky substance

retreat: place where a person goes to relax

Scandinavian: involving a region of northern Europe that includes the countries of Norway, Sweden, and Denmark; Finland and Iceland are sometimes included, too

voice-activated: machine that begins working after a person speaks

Where to Learn More

More Books to Read

Croft, Peter. *Clay Shooting: A Complete Guide to Skeet, Trap and Sporting Shooting*. London: Ward Lock, 1990.

Haugen, Brenda. *Annie Oakley: American Sharpshooter*. Minneapolis: Compass Point Books, 2007.

On the Road

World Shooting & Recreational Complex
1 Main Event Lane
Sparta, IL 62286
618/295-2700

On the Web

For more information on this topic, use FactHound.

1. Go to *www.facthound.com*
2. Type in this book ID: 0756538653
3. Click on the *Fetch It* button.

FactHound will find the best Web sites for you.

INDEX

ABOUT THE AUTHOR

Shane Frederick is a sportswriter who lives in Mankato, Minnesota, with his wife, Sara, and three children, Ben, Jack, and Lucy. He covers college hockey and recreational sports for *The Free Press* newspaper. He enjoys music, drawing, tennis, and curling.